Dream Hatching

LIGHT RAIN
PUBLISHING

Light Rain Publishing
© Constance Mears 2016
ISBN 978-0-9982409-0-9 Hardcover
ISBN 978-0-9982409-3-0 Softcover

All rights reserved.
No part of this book may be reproduced in any form without written permission from the author.
www.constancemears.com

BRING YOUR DREAM TO LIFE

CONSTANCE MEARS

INTRODUCTION

Each of us has a Dream for our life: something we want to do or be that feels exciting and maybe even a little scary. We can spend our life ignoring it, pretending it doesn't matter. We can stay busy. We can let life pull us in other directions, but now and then our Dream still calls to us.

That Dream, tucked away in our hearts, will stay with us for 10, 20, even 50 years. It's not going away. We don't want to get to the end of the line and realize we never went for it, we never "brought it to life."

Each day we have the chance to nurture our Dream or neglect it, to play it safe or muster the courage to take the next step.

And here's the beautiful secret: as we bring our Dream to life, our Dream brings us to life—we come to embody the deepest, richest version of ourselves.

DREAM HATCHING | CONSTANCE MEARS

BE VISIONARY

"Every great dream begins with a Dreamer."
HARRIET TUBMAN

Get your head out of the clouds—isn't that what they told you? Come back down to earth. Stop dreaming. Get real. How many of those messages did you hear, until you could no longer hear your Dream's call?

Well, my friend, here is your invitation to get back in those clouds, so you can get a bird's-eye view of your life. Let your mind wander, rising above your present-day concerns.

What themes keep surfacing? What possibilities get your spirit soaring?

For now, just allow yourself to be a high-flying Dreamer.

DREAM HATCHING | CONSTANCE MEARS

MIGRATE

"That which you seek is seeking you."
Rumi

You've got to love a species that invented the idea of flying south for the winter. As a rule, birds seek out environments that fully support them. They fly in the opposite direction of storms. They don't try to "weather" inhospitable situations. When things get dark, they seek brighter horizons, putting distance between themselves and stressful circumstances.

When birds set out, they may not even know where they're headed, but they trust their instincts. They trust their inner GPS.

What environment could you migrate toward that will support you in thriving?

DREAM HATCHING | CONSTANCE MEARS

FIND YOUR FLOCK

"If you want to go fast, go alone.
If you want to go far, go together."
AFRICAN PROVERB

Finding your flock is not about conforming; it's about finding people who "get" you, who celebrate you, who support you in being your most authentic, quirky self. They're your peeps.

In flock mentality, a bird takes off in a direction and other birds fall in behind. The bird in the first position is not a set leader. When it gets tired, and it will—because the lead position is the most taxing—it drops back and lets another bird move forward. There's no skirmish or power struggle.

If ever a bird senses another direction or route would be better, it simply breaks off from the flock. Sometimes other birds follow, sometimes not.

Find your flock, fly together, but always, always follow your heart.

DREAM HATCHING | CONSTANCE MEARS

SELF-REFLECTION

"Midlife is when you reach the top of the ladder only to discover it's leaning against the wrong wall."
JOSEPH CAMPBELL

In the children's fable "The Ugly Duckling" by Hans Christian Andersen, a beautiful swan feels like an odd duck, because she doesn't match others' expectations. She tones down her best qualities so she can fit in. One day she catches her reflection in the lake and sees her beauty for the first time.

Don't let others define who you are, what you're worth, or who you can become. Take time for self-reflection and discover your unique gifts and qualities. Be yourself, even if others don't understand. Soon you'll attract a flock that values you for who you are.

Have you been playing small, so as not to ruffle someone else's feathers?

DREAM HATCHING | CONSTANCE MEARS

THE CAGED BIRD

"The doors to the world of the wild Self are few but precious. If you have a deep scar, that is a door, if you have an old, old story, that is a door. If you love the sky and the water so much you almost cannot bear it, that is a door. If you yearn for a deeper life, a full life, a sane life, that is a door."

CLARISSA PINKOLA ESTÉS,
WOMEN WHO RUN WITH THE WOLVES

Your soul longs for an expanse of wild, blue sky. It remembers how good the breeze feels on your outstretched wings. It knows the song you came here to sing.

If your Dreams are barren, you may have become overly domesticated. Begin by re-wilding yourself. Wander off for an afternoon. Spread your wings. Become a free-range Dreamer. There's a whole world waiting right outside your door.

DREAM HATCHING | CONSTANCE MEARS

COMMIT

You don't need all the answers, all the resources, all the courage for the entire journey before you start. If you wait for it all, you will never begin.

Once you commit to the journey, you need only enough energy, focus, and heart to overcome inertia. Choose to commit right now.

"Until one is committed,
there is hesitancy, the chance to draw back,
always ineffectiveness. Concerning
all acts of initiative (and creation),
there is one elementary truth
the ignorance of which kills countless ideas
and splendid plans: that the moment
one definitely commits oneself,
then Providence moves, too.
All sorts of things occur to help one that
would never otherwise have occurred."
WILLIAM MURRAY, FIRST PERSON TO SUMMIT MT. EVEREST

DREAM HATCHING | CONSTANCE MEARS

BE INSPIRED

*"Let silence take you
to the core of life."*
Rumi

Winter strips away the dead wood, that which no longer bears fruit. Its wild storms leave a blank canvas upon which to create. As any artist knows, the blank slate may look empty, but it's packed with possibilities.

Clear some blank space in your mind, your home, your heart, and your calendar. Exhale deeply, so you can be "inspired." Let go of old ideas to make room for fresh growth.

Winter's quiet allows you to hear what's calling to be born through you. Resist the urge to drown out silence. It may have something important to tell you.

DREAM HATCHING | CONSTANCE MEARS

TUNE IN TO NATURE'S RHYTHM

*"The imagination needs moodling
—long, inefficient happy idling,
dawdling and puttering."*
BRENDA UELAND

Nature's rhythm moves differently than the clang, clang, clang of our nonstop culture. A Dream may ebb and flow, molt, go dormant, then suddenly spring to life.

We may be tempted to bypass certain stages in the creative cycle, because it seems as if nothing is happening. Nature knows better.

Give yourself the gifts of: silence, dormancy, sleep, unplugging, long walks, bubble baths, lounging, dreaming, doodling, moodling, dawdling, and going deep within.

Tune in to your own natural rhythms.

DREAM HATCHING | CONSTANCE MEARS

FIND YOUR VOICE

*I*n the bird world, everybody sings.
There are no celebrity birds, or birds with "great voices" that sing for the whole flock. Every bird finds its own authentic expression, and together, they create a symphony of collaboration, and deep-forest jam sessions.

Every bird sings its own song, not what's most popular. They sing with abandon, throwing back their heads to greet the day, and as a closing ceremony when evening comes.

Singing is one of the ways birds find each other. How will your flock find you if they don't hear your song?

> "...the only way to find your voice
> is to use it. It's hardwired, built into you.
> Talk about the things you love,
> and your voice will follow."
>
> AUSTIN KLEON

DREAM HATCHING | CONSTANCE MEARS

CALL AND RESPONSE

In the bird world, the male bird tries to impress females with the volume and variety of his calls. Females show their receptiveness by calling back.

In Dream Hatching, we listen for a strong "calling"—themes that keep surfacing, that speak to our heart. Life is courting us with purposeful adventure. If we are receptive, and willing to bring our Dreams into being—to give them form, to give them life—we answer the call.

You can think of this as co-creating with the Divine, or a Muse, God, the Universe, or a Higher Power. We offer ourselves as the conduit through which new creation can emerge.

What has been calling to you? If you are receptive, and up for the adventure, respond with a hearty YES!

DREAM HATCHING | CONSTANCE MEARS

A SACRED PARTNERSHIP

"The union of the Feminine and Masculine within the individual is the basis of all creation."
SHAKTI GAWAN

As we respond to Life's invitation, our Dream elevates to a "calling."

Dream Hatching consciously combines the Feminine and Masculine. Out of that union, a Dream is conceived. We don't chase our Dream, we birth it.

In Dream Hatching, we embody the Sacred Feminine – not the hyper-sexualized cultural version, but by offering to bring new creation into being through us. We honor the regenerative, intuitive, emotional, cooperative, nurturing, and receptive qualities.

Like human procreation, co-creation takes only a few minutes to initiate. It may be weeks before any outward signs begin to show, but something new is coming into being.

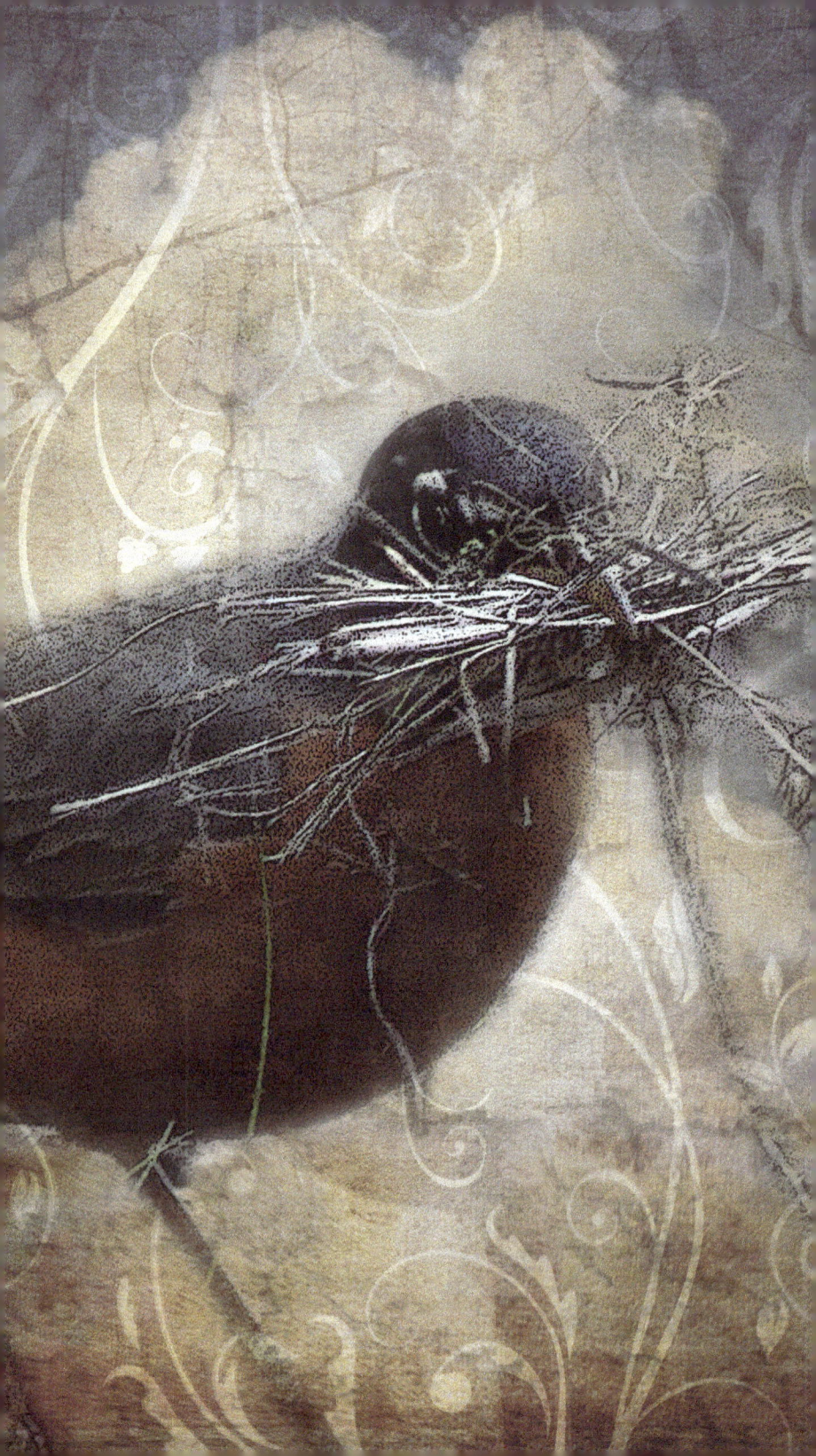

FEEL THE QUICKENING

When you "conceive" an idea in sacred partnership with Life, you become pregnant with possibilities. You are literally in a state of expecting.

You may feel a mixture of excitement and fear. Your heart quickens to realize that your Dream could actually come to life.

> "We all begin the process
> before we are ready, before we are strong
> enough, before we know enough;
> we begin a dialogue with thoughts and
> feelings that both tickle and thunder
> within us. We respond before we know
> how to speak the language, before we know
> all the answers, and before we know
> exactly to whom we are speaking."
> — Clarissa Pinkola Estes

DREAM HATCHING | CONSTANCE MEARS

CREATE SPACE

*I*f we're serious about hatching our Dream, we have to create space for it. A bird doesn't wait until the eggs are laid to begin making a nest, just like a couple doesn't wait until the baby is born to put the nursery together. Birds don't wait to see how big the eggs are, or how many likes they'll get on Facebook.

Clear that guest room, take that class, act as if good things are on the way. Create a nest big enough to support your Dream until it gets off the ground.

Carve out time in your schedule, too. Give your embryonic Dream a chance to find its form.

Here's another reason to find your flock: If you're starting to build an eagle's nest, but you're hanging out with crows, you may get flak from your flock. Their disapproving looks or comments may cause you to second-guess your instincts. What feels right to others, may not work for you.

Create space for that which hasn't come into being yet.

DREAM HATCHING | CONSTANCE MEARS

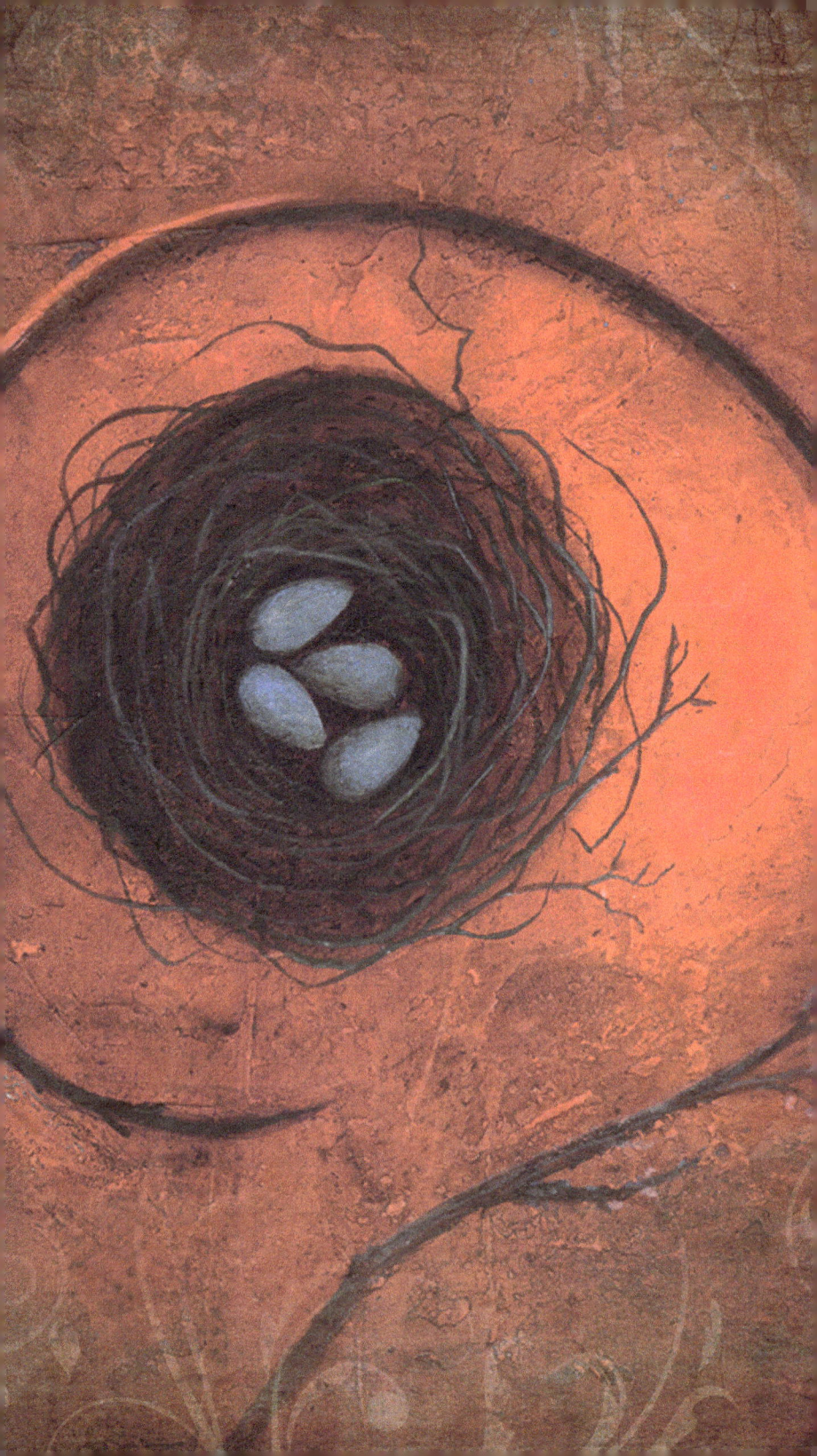

GESTATION

"Faith is a place of mystery, where we find the courage to believe in what we cannot see and the strength to let go of our fear of uncertainty."

Brené Brown

Like all adventures, Dream Hatching requires courage. The root of the word "courage" is from the old French "corage" and the Latin "cor," which both mean heart. The essential quality of a Dream is its heart.

We need to sit with our embryonic Dream when it's just a few swirly ideas. Soon enough, a heartbeat begins. Thump-thump, thump-thump. Our Dream is now connected to the Life Force.

We resist the urge to crack the egg, so we can organize, monitor, or orchestrate its development. We resist the urge to rush it so we have something to show others for our time and effort. Our job is to sit with it, love it, allow it to gestate.

THE BROOD PATCH

During gestation, birds develop what's called a "brood patch." Feathers in the chest area come loose, exposing the heart. This allows the heart to transfer heat directly to the egg.

Exposing the heart—choosing vulnerability—requires a different kind of courage than the warrior's courage, where one shields the heart.

This work of sitting with, being present, giving attention to something remains undervalued in our action-based culture, but the most important thing you can do during this stage is to give your whole heart to your embryonic Dream.

When mama birds sit on their eggs, they wiggle a little, settling in so the brood patch makes full contact with the egg.

Have you settled into your Dream yet,
or are you still only "half-hearted?"

DREAM HATCHING | CONSTANCE MEARS

DEVELOP BOUNDARIES

Birds build nests in hard to reach places and their eggs come with hard shells and clever camouflage.

Not everyone who shows an interest in your Dream has your best interests at heart. Beware of predators, even well-meaning friends, who can shatter your Dream with one blunt comment.

Or take cowbirds, for example. They lays their eggs in other birds' nests, letting others do all the work.

Do you have any cowbirds in your life? People who drop things in your lap? People whose big Dreams are fueled by your effort, leaving less for your own Dream? Look at your nest. Look at your calendar. Are those your eggs?

> You can't set a boundary and take care of someone else's feelings at the same time.
>
> ANNE KATHERINE, BOUNDARIES

COMING OUT OF YOUR SHELL

"...if a person has had the sense of the Call –
the feeling that there's an adventure
for him [or her] – and if she doesn't follow that,
but remains in the society because it's safe
and secure, then life dries up.
JOSEPH CAMPBELL

Yes, we have risked being Dreamers, but we can't stop there. This is the principle of transformation: to let go of what is, so that something new can emerge.

A hatchling has a temporary point on its beak called an egg tooth, that helps it break the shell. It looks for the light—the place where the shell is thinnest—which is the path of least resistance. This approach uses its resources most efficiently.

Your Dream will have time to grow once it gets "out there," but for now, look for the brightest opportunity. Use your egg tooth and chip away.

DREAM HATCHING | CONSTANCE MEARS

FALLING APART

Often a breakdown comes just before the breakthrough.

It may feel as if things are falling apart, or that we are "cracking up." We can expend a lot of energy trying to keep it all together, but sometimes falling apart **is** the next step in our transformation.

Sometimes things fall away to let something new emerge.

Don't worry. Breathe deeply and trust that all is well. The world loves a feisty hatchling that can overcome obstacles.

> "When a lot of things start going wrong all at once, it is to protect something big and lovely that is trying to get itself born...."
> ANNE LAMOTT, QUOTING WISDOM FROM THE DALAI LAMA

DREAM HATCHING | CONSTANCE MEARS

STAY WITH IT

Newly hatched Dreams start small.

Many people abandon their Dream as soon as it hatches, because it doesn't match the image of how they thought it should look. Often people feel embarrassed. They think they must have made a mistake when this gangly, awkward little Dream shows up:

    That first workshop where only one person came.
    A first date after our divorce.
    Those early paintings, drafts, riffs that we reject outright because they don't compare to the masterworks of others.

It may not look like the soaring Dream we've been imagining, but stay with it. Don't let it grow cold. Feed it and feed it and feed it some more. Give your Dream time to find its wings.

DREAM HATCHING | CONSTANCE MEARS

CHERISH THE PRESENT

Once your Dream hatches, it will require more time, resources, and energy than you ever imagined. Now is the time for the to-do lists and multi-tasking. You might lose sleep, forget to eat, or feel overwhelmed. That's OK. It's all part of the process. One day soon you'll notice the load has lightened a little.

In the meantime, remember to appreciate the ordinary moments: the feel of the breeze on your face; the chirps and peeps of little ones; the feeling of accomplishment in having brought your Dream to life.

You may feel as if you're always running behind, but you're way ahead of those who haven't even started yet.

> "The present moment, if you think about it, is the only time there is. No matter what time it is, it is always now."
> MARIANNE WILLIAMSON

DREAM HATCHING | CONSTANCE MEARS

ABUNDANCE

"If you have the guts to follow the risk,
life opens, opens, opens up all along the line.
I'm not superstitious, but I do believe
in spiritual magic, you might say.
I feel that if one follows what I call one's 'bliss'
—the thing that really gets you deep in the
gut and that you feel is your life—doors will
open up. They do! They have in my life and
they have in many lives that I know of."

JOSEPH CAMPBELL

Yes, the early bird gets the worm. And so does the late bird, and the midday bird. Nature is abundant. Tune in to your natural instincts to find the resources you need. Did you miss the juicy worm? That's OK. There are gnats and grubs and seeds.

Birds don't stockpile for the future. That's one thing that keeps them "free as a bird." Trust that all you need will be provided, when you need it.

DREAM HATCHING | CONSTANCE MEARS

TAKE THE LEAP

In the fledgling stage, we find out what our Dream is made of, and if its heart—its courage— is strong.

So far, our Dream has been coddled and nurtured, but now it's time to get it off the ground. The launch is when we may need to watch our baby take a few tumbles.

Be patient with your fears. Leaping into the unknown, doing something for the first time, can feel daunting— even impossible.

100% of flying happens outside the nest. Our Dream can't soar until we get it out of its comfort zone, no matter how long it took us to create it.

We find our wings on the way down.

"Feel the fear, and do it anyway."
SUSAN JEFFERS

DREAM HATCHING | CONSTANCE MEARS

SOARING

The word "original" stems from the Latin "oriri," which means "to rise."

While eagles don't technically "migrate," they often fly many miles to find abundant habitats. They can't get where they need to go using only their own power; they would become exhausted soon after starting out. Instead, they learn to catch thermals, invisible currents of warm air that are present only at higher levels. Here, they can soar up to 75 mph, without even flapping their wings.

Be an original. Let the thermals—blessings, synchronicity, miracles and manifestations— carry you higher than you ever dreamed possible.

"Don't be satisfied with stories, how things have gone with others. Unfold your own myth."

RUMI

DREAM HATCHING | CONSTANCE MEARS

TREASURE THE UNEXPECTED

*"Keep some room in your heart
for the unimaginable."*
MARY OLIVER

Oh, it's one thing to map out a to-do list, follow a recipe to the half-teaspoon, and color inside the lines. That's called mastery. But life takes on a bit of the magical when you open yourself to be surprised and delighted. That's called mystery.

For some, living in the Mystery feels uncomfortable, unpredictable, and unsettling, but you can condition your "miracle muscle" just like the muscles in your body.

The first step is to ask! Instead of "making it happen," with your willpower, wit and wiles, try letting something come to you instead. Try it out on something that isn't make-or-break. Often the answer shows up in an unexpected form that you call a terrible mistake. Then the light catches it, and it sparkles—and suddenly you realize you've been given a treasure.

DREAM HATCHING | CONSTANCE MEARS

SOLITUDE

*"Only when one is connected
to one's own core is one connected
to others, I am beginning to discover.
And for me, the core, the inner spring,
can best be refound through solitude."*
Anne Morrow Lindbergh, Gift From the Sea

We may have found our flock, but we still need time for solitude.

Only when we immerse ourselves, do we find that source of deep replenishment. Yes, developing a rich inner life takes time, but it quenches our soul's thirst for meaning.

Love of solitude doesn't come naturally to every one, but we can gradually build up to a few minutes a day. Without distractions and outside influences, we can more easily catch a vision of our soul's deepest expression.

DREAM HATCHING | CONSTANCE MEARS

THE EMPTY NEST

"Fall seven times, get up eight."
CHINESE PROVERB

*L*oss is part of the journey, too.

To create from the heart is to be vulnerable to loss. When you bring anything to life, it becomes bound by the cycle of life, death, and rebirth. You can't avoid the risk of loss by not creating. In doing so, you experience an even greater loss—your unborn Dream.

Along the way, you may encounter setbacks or hardships. During these times, you find out who your flock is. Let their love bring you back to life.

Loss is inevitable, and often makes us stronger than we ever knew was possible.

DREAM HATCHING | CONSTANCE MEARS

MANAGING MOMENTUM

"When you're that successful, things have momentum, and at a certain point, you can't really tell whether you have created the momentum or it's creating you."
— ANNIE LENNOX

Once your Dream gets off the ground, the velocity increases until one day you realize you need to hit the brakes.

Learning to land gracefully is just as important as learning to fly. It's exciting to have your head in the clouds, but coming back down to earth keeps us grounded.

While things are still flying high, study the terrain for a soft place to land. Self-care means giving yourself time to descend instead of crash landing in a free-fall of panic. Envision—and ask for—smooth transitions!

CELEBRATE THE JOURNEY

Life should not only be lived,
it should be celebrated.
Osho

Take time to mark the milestones. Find your flock and celebrate how far you've come.

Tell your stories. Share and honor both the highlights and difficulties. Look for things to celebrate, and you'll find them everywhere.

Celebrate with music, with laughter, with children and elders. Celebrate with nourishing food in beautiful settings. Celebrate the success of others. Practice the art of celebration.

DREAM HATCHING | CONSTANCE MEARS

SYNCHRONICITY

"Why, sometimes I've believed as many as six impossible things before breakfast."
Alice in Wonderland, by Lewis Carroll

When I started writing Dream Hatching, I asked for an example of how co-creating works.

The first step is to ask, and to believe what we're asking is possible, even if we don't know the how of it yet.

If I couldn't get something amazing to happen—right here, right now—I had no business suggesting this process to others. So I asked for something unlikely to happen on the subject of synchronicity.

I sat in my car at the park writing, when a few minutes later two eagles flew overhead. While rare, that wasn't unlikely, but then they lined up and flew in synch together. They flew with wings outspread, then tucked deftly close to their bodies, in what amounted to an impromptu show of aerial dynamics.

RENEWAL

Creation moves in cycles. First the idea, then commitment. Next comes finding or creating the optimum circumstances in which your Dream can thrive. Then we open ourselves to a co-creation, hearing a "call" and responding with a hearty yes. We sit with our embryonic Dream, giving it time to find its heart and its form, until one day it hatches of its own timing. We stay with our vulnerable Dream, trusting that it will grow into the vision we've been inspired by.

More smply put, Dream Hatching is the process of making love with Life, with the Creative Life Force that inhabits all living things. We tap into that immense power to bring something new into being. In this context, we don't birth a human being, we birth a project, an experience, a quality—which often also contributes to the well-being of others. In this way, not only do we thrive in the bearing of our gifts, but our ties to community are strengthened as well.

It all starts with Dreaming.

DREAM HATCHING | CONSTANCE MEARS

DREAM BIG

"If you limit your choices only to what seems possible or reasonable, you disconnect yourself from what you truly want, and all that is left is compromise."

Anaïs Nin

Your ego's ambitions generally involve some level of fame or fortune. Soul Dreams, on the other hand, generally focus on meaning and contribution.

When you factor in the participation of Providence, you aren't limited to only low-hanging, reasonable Dreams. What I've experienced in my own life is that the higher and juicier the Dream, the higher I'm lifted to reach it.

Dream Big and count on those thermals. The world needs the contribution you came here to make.

DREAM HATCHING | CONSTANCE MEARS

ACKNOWLEDGEMENTS

Heartfelt appreciation goes to:
book coach Crystal Stranaghan at CCS-Crystal Clear Solutions; my peeps, Ben and Jackie Mears; Peggi Erickson for inspiration, feedback, and friendship; my parents Chuck and Genevieve Mears and siblings for familial love and support; designer Ana Fagarazzi and AF Studios for the lovely texture. But most of all, to Creator for the life and gifts I've been given.

> "There is a vitality, a Life Force, a quickening
> that is translated through you into action,
> and because there is only one of you
> in all time, this expression is unique.
> If you block it, it will never exist
> through any other medium.
> It will be lost.
> The world will not have it."
> MARTHA GRAHAM

ABOUT THE AUTHOR

As an artist, a writer, mystic and creator of Dream Hatching, Constance Mears is familiar with the creative process. She offers workshops for women who want to clarify their dreams and bring them to life. She lives along an inlet in Port Orchard, WA, where she paints, writes, and takes bird photos, some of which appear in this book. Currently, she is polishing her spiritual memoir, The Bumbling Mystic's Obituary.

ABOUT THE IMAGES

Most images in this book began with photos taken by Constance of local birds, over the course of two years. Images for egg hatching, robin with babies, and fledging owl started with stock images. These photos are then digitally enhanced and blended with layers of clouds and textures.

Find out more at www.constancemears.com

www.ingramcontent.com/pod-product-compliance
Lightning Source LLC
Chambersburg PA
CBHW041108160426
42811CB00091B/1108